NO FISH MEDITERRANEAN DIET

Savory recipes for health conscious foodies and those

with fish allergies

Wendy S. Laine

TABLE OF CONTENT

CHAPTER ONE

Introduction

Welcome to the world of Mediterranean cuisine, a vibrant and flavorful culinary journey that captures the essence of sun-soaked coastlines, lush olive groves, and centuries-old traditions. In this unique cookbook, we invite you to explore the tantalizing world of Mediterranean flavors without a single fish in sight. We've curated a collection of delectable recipes that celebrate the diverse and bountiful Mediterranean region, offering you a rich tapestry of dishes inspired by its diverse cultures and climates.

Overview of Mediterranean Cuisine

Mediterranean cuisine is renowned not only for its exceptional taste but also for its health benefits. This diet is more than just a way of eating; it's a lifestyle that promotes overall well-being. At its core, Mediterranean cuisine emphasizes fresh and whole ingredients, emphasizing the use of fruits, vegetables, legumes, grains, and heart-healthy fats like olive oil. Rich in antioxidants, vitamins, and minerals, this cuisine is a powerhouse of nutrients that can support a healthier lifestyle.

Benefits of a Mediterranean Diet without Fish

By choosing to focus on a Mediterranean diet that excludes fish, you're embarking on a journey that offers numerous health advantages. This cookbook will show you how to derive all the benefits of the Mediterranean diet while adhering to your dietary preferences. Expect to enjoy improved heart health, better weight management, reduced risk of chronic diseases, and increased longevity. With the right combination of ingredients and flavors, you can savor all the goodness of Mediterranean cuisine without compromising your dietary choices.

How to Use This Cookbook

Navigating this cookbook is a breeze, whether you're an experienced cook or a novice in the kitchen. Each recipe is thoughtfully crafted with clear, step-by-step instructions that are easy to follow. We've also provided serving suggestions and tips to enhance your culinary experience. Whether you're looking for a quick and healthy weeknight meal or planning an impressive dinner for guests, you'll find the perfect recipe within these pages.

CHAPTER TWO

Getting started

Before you dive into the world of Mediterranean flavors, we'll help you get started on the right foot. Chapter 1 provides you with essential insights into the ingredients commonly used in Mediterranean cuisine, offering guidance on where to source them and how to select the best quality produce. You'll discover the key herbs, spices, and pantry staples that infuse Mediterranean dishes with their distinctive character.

As you embark on this culinary journey through the Mediterranean, prepare to unlock a world of delicious, nourishing, and satisfying dishes. From aromatic soups to hearty stews, vibrant salads, and comforting starchy creations, this cookbook is your passport to the heart of Mediterranean gastronomy. Get ready to savor the Mediterranean, one mouthwatering bite at a time.

Essential Ingredients in the Mediterranean Pantry

A well-stocked Mediterranean pantry is the foundation for creating delicious and authentic dishes without fish. Here are some essential ingredients you should have on hand:

Extra Virgin Olive Oil: Olive oil is the cornerstone of Mediterranean cooking, and it remains a key ingredient for flavor, even in fish-free dishes. It's used for sautéing, roasting, drizzling, and dressing salads.

Herbs and Spices: Mediterranean cuisine relies on a variety of herbs and spices to add flavor. Common options include oregano, basil, thyme, rosemary, parsley, garlic, cumin, paprika, and coriander.

Fresh Vegetables: Stock up on a variety of fresh vegetables such as tomatoes, bell peppers, eggplant, zucchini, onions, garlic, and leafy greens like spinach.

Legumes: Mediterranean dishes often feature legumes like chickpeas, lentils, and white beans. They are versatile and packed with protein and fiber.

Grains: Common grains include rice, bulgur, couscous, and pasta. These form the base of many Mediterranean recipes.

Canned Tomatoes: Canned tomatoes, especially crushed or diced, are essential for making sauces and soups.

Olives: Mediterranean olives come in various types, such as Kalamata, green, and black. They are used in salads, spreads, and as garnishes.

Nuts: Almonds, walnuts, and pine nuts add texture and flavor to Mediterranean dishes. They are often used in salads, pilafs, and desserts.

Cheeses: Feta, goat cheese, and Parmesan are common Mediterranean cheeses used for their unique flavors and textures.

Vinegars: Red wine vinegar and balsamic vinegar are used for salad dressings and marinades.

Honey: Natural honey is used to sweeten desserts, dressings, and drizzled over cheese.

Dried Fruits: Mediterranean recipes often incorporate dried fruits like raisins, apricots, and figs for sweetness and texture.

Canned Legumes: Canned chickpeas and beans offer convenience and are perfect for quick Mediterranean meals.

Kitchen Tools and Equipment

To successfully prepare Mediterranean dishes without fish, having the right kitchen tools and equipment can make a significant difference. Here's a list of essential items:

Chef's Knife: A good-quality chef's knife is crucial for chopping, slicing, and dicing vegetables and herbs.

Cutting Board: Use a sturdy cutting board to protect your countertops and make food prep more manageable.

Saute Pan: A versatile sauté pan is perfect for cooking vegetables, legumes, and creating flavorful sauces.

Dutch oven: A heavy-duty Dutch oven is ideal for slow-cooked Mediterranean stews and braised dishes.

Baking Sheet: Baking sheets are handy for roasting vegetables and making flatbreads.

Blender or Food Processor: These appliances are essential for making sauces, dips, and purées.

Grater: Use a grater for cheese, citrus zest, and nutmeg.

Salad Spinner: A salad spinner helps you wash and dry greens and herbs thoroughly.

Measuring Cups and Spoons: Precise measurements are essential for baking and cooking.

Sieve or Strainer: Use these for rinsing canned beans and draining pasta.

Peeler: A vegetable peeler is handy for peeling potatoes, carrots, and cucumbers.

Wooden Spoons: Wooden spoons are gentle on cookware and are great for stirring sauces.

Basic Cooking Techniques

Mediterranean cuisine relies on simple yet effective cooking techniques to enhance flavors and create satisfying dishes without fish:

Sautéing: Sautéing vegetables, garlic, and onions in olive oil is a common starting point for many Mediterranean dishes.

Roasting: Roasting brings out the natural sweetness in vegetables and intensifies their flavors. It's often used for tomatoes, peppers, eggplant, and more.

Grilling: Grilling adds a smoky and charred flavor to vegetables and plant-based proteins.

Braising: Braising is a slow-cooking method that combines searing and simmering, creating tender and flavorful dishes like Mediterranean stews.

Simmering: Simmering is used for cooking grains, legumes, and sauces to allow flavors to meld.

Blending: Blending is essential for creating smooth soups, dips, and sauces, like the classic Mediterranean hummus.

Dressing: Learning to make simple vinaigrettes and dressings is key for Mediterranean salads.

Marinating: Marinating vegetables and plant-based proteins in olive oil and herbs infuses them with flavor before cooking.

Mastering these techniques and having the right ingredients and tools at your disposal will empower you to create a wide range of delightful Mediterranean dishes without fish, offering you a journey through flavors that are not only delicious but also healthy and satisfying.

CHAPTER THREE

BREAKFAST

Mango Smoothie

Ingredients

- 2 ripe mangoes, peeled and chopped
- 1/2 cup coconut milk
- 1/2 teaspoon vanilla extract

1 cup Greek yogurt

1 tablespoon honey (or to taste)

Ice cubes (optional)

Instructions

1. In a blender, combine the chopped mangoes, Greek yogurt, coconut milk, honey, and vanilla extract.
2. Blend until smooth. If the smoothie is too thick, add a little more coconut milk or water to reach your desired consistency.
3. Taste and adjust sweetness with additional honey if needed.
4. For a colder smoothie, add a few ice cubes and blend until smooth.
5. Serve immediately in tall glasses.

Estimated Nutritional Value (per serving)

Calories: ~200-250, Protein: 6-8g, Carbohydrates: 45-50g, Fat: 3-5g

For a vegan version, substitute Greek yogurt with a plant-based yogurt and honey with maple syrup or agave nectar.

You can add a scoop of protein powder for an extra protein boost.

Mediterranean Sandwiches

Ingredients

- 4 whole wheat sandwich bread slices
- 1 ripe tomato, sliced
- 1/4 cup fresh basil leaves
- 2 tablespoons sriracha-mayo pesto (combine 1 tbsp. sriracha sauce with 2 tbsp. mayonnaise and 1 tbsp. pesto)
- Olive oil for brushing

1/2 cup feta cheese, crumbled

1/2 cucumber, thinly sliced

Instructions

1. Lightly brush one side of each bread slice with olive oil.
2. Spread the sriracha-mayo pesto on the non-oiled side of two bread slices.
3. Layer feta cheese, tomato slices, cucumber slices, and fresh basil on top of the pesto.
4. Close the sandwiches with the remaining bread slices, oiled side facing out.
5. Heat a grill pan or sandwich press over medium heat.
6. Grill the sandwiches for 3-4 minutes on each side or until golden and crispy.

7. Cut diagonally and serve warm.

Estimated Nutritional Value (per serving):

Calories: ~350-400, Protein: 12-15g, Carbohydrates: 35-40g, Fat: 18-22g

Substitute whole wheat bread with any other whole grain bread for variation.

Add grilled chicken or turkey slices for added protein.

Healthy Breakfast Egg Muffins

Ingredients

- 6 large eggs
- 1 cup spinach, chopped
- 1/4 cup onions, finely chopped
- 1/4 cup feta cheese, crumbled
- Cooking spray or olive oil

1/2 cup milk (dairy or plant-based)

1/2 bell pepper, diced

1/2 cup cherry tomatoes, halved

Salt and pepper to taste

Instructions

1. Preheat the oven to 375°F (190°C). Grease a muffin tin with cooking spray or olive oil.

2. In a large bowl, whisk together eggs and milk. Season with salt and pepper.

3. Stir in spinach, bell pepper, onions, cherry tomatoes, and feta cheese.

4. Pour the egg mixture evenly into the muffin tin.

5. Bake for 20-25 minutes, or until the tops are firm to the touch and eggs are cooked.

6. Allow to cool for a few minutes before removing from the tin.

7. Serve warm or store in the refrigerator for up to 4 days.

Estimated Nutritional Value (per muffin):

Calories: ~100-120, Protein: 6-8g, Carbohydrates: 3-5g, Fat: 7-9g

Experiment with different vegetables like zucchini, mushrooms, or asparagus.

For a dairy-free version, omit the cheese or use a dairy-free cheese alternative.

Grilled Mango with Lime, Aleppo Pepper, and Honey

Ingredients

- 2 ripe mangoes, peeled and sliced into thick strips
- 1 tablespoon olive oil   1 lime, juiced and zested

- 2 tablespoons honey   A pinch of salt
- 1/2 teaspoon Aleppo pepper (or substitute with a mild chili powder)
- Fresh mint leaves for garnish (optional)

Instructions

1. Preheat a grill or grill pan over medium heat.
2. Brush the mango slices lightly with olive oil to prevent sticking.
3. Grill the mango slices for about 2-3 minutes on each side, or until they have nice grill marks and are slightly softened.
4. In a small bowl, whisk together the lime juice, lime zest, honey, Aleppo pepper, and a pinch of salt.
5. Arrange the grilled mango slices on a serving plate. Drizzle the lime and honey mixture over the grilled mango.
6. Garnish with fresh mint leaves if desired.
7. Serve immediately while warm.

Type of Cuisine: Mediterranean-Inspired Fusion

Estimated Nutritional Value (per serving):

Calories: Approximately 120-150, Protein: 1g, Carbohydrates: 28-32g, Fat: 2-3g

If Aleppo pepper is not available, a mix of smoked paprika and a pinch of cayenne pepper can be a good substitute.

Ensure the mangoes are ripe but firm enough to hold their shape when grilled.

For a vegan version, substitute honey with maple syrup or agave nectar.

Healthy Blueberry Muffins (Whole Wheat)

Ingredients

- 1 3/4 cups whole wheat flour
- 1/3 cup raw sugar or honey
- 1/2 teaspoon baking soda
- 1 teaspoon ground cinnamon
- 2 large eggs
- 1/4 cup olive oil or melted coconut oil
- Zest of 1 lemon (optional)

1/2 cup rolled oats

2 teaspoons baking powder

1/2 teaspoon salt

1 cup fresh blueberries

1 cup plain Greek yogurt

1 teaspoon vanilla extract

Instructions

1. Preheat the oven to 375°F (190°C). Line a muffin tin with paper liners or lightly grease with cooking spray.
2. In a large bowl, combine whole wheat flour, rolled oats, sugar (or honey), baking powder, baking soda, salt, and cinnamon. Gently stir in the blueberries.
3. In another bowl, whisk together eggs, Greek yogurt, oil, vanilla extract, and lemon zest (if using) until well combined.
4. Add the wet ingredients to the dry ingredients and mix just until combined. Be careful not to overmix.
5. Spoon the batter into the prepared muffin tin, filling each cup about 3/4 full.
6. Bake for 20-25 minutes, or until a toothpick inserted into the center of a muffin comes out clean.
7. Remove from the oven and let the muffins cool in the pan for 5 minutes, then transfer to a wire rack to cool completely.

Estimated Nutritional Value (per muffin):

Calories: Approximately 150-180, Protein: 4-6g, Carbohydrates: 22-26g, Fat: 6-8g

You can replace half of the whole wheat flour with all-purpose flour for a lighter texture.

If using frozen blueberries, do not thaw them before adding to the batter to prevent bleeding.

Add nuts like chopped walnuts or almonds for an added crunch and nutritional boost.

Eggs with Summer Tomatoes, Zucchini, and Bell Peppers

Ingredients

- 4 large eggs
- 1 bell pepper (color of your choice), diced
- 1 small onion, finely chopped
- 2 tablespoons olive oil
- Fresh herbs (such as basil or parsley), for garnish
- Crumbled feta cheese (optional)

1 medium zucchini, thinly sliced

2 medium tomatoes, chopped

2 cloves of garlic, minced

Salt and pepper to taste

Instructions

1. Heat olive oil in a large skillet over medium heat. Add the onion and garlic, sautéing until the onion is translucent.

2. Add the bell pepper and zucchini to the skillet. Cook for about 5 minutes, or until they start to soften.

3. Stir in the chopped tomatoes and cook for another 3-4 minutes, until the tomatoes release their juices.

4. Make four wells in the vegetable mixture and crack an egg into each well. Season with salt and pepper.

5. Cover the skillet with a lid and cook over low heat until the eggs are cooked to your desired doneness (about 4-6 minutes for soft yolks).

6. Garnish with fresh herbs and crumbled feta cheese if desired.

7. Serve hot, straight from the skillet.

Estimated Nutritional Value (per serving):

Calories: Approximately 200-250, Protein: 12-15g, Carbohydrates: 8-10g, Fat: 15-17gTips:

For an extra kick of flavor, add a pinch of smoked paprika or cayenne pepper.

You can substitute zucchini and bell peppers with other seasonal vegetables like spinach, asparagus, or mushrooms.

For a dairy-free version, omit the feta cheese or use a dairy-free cheese alternative.

Avocado and Egg Breakfast Pizza

Ingredients

- 1 whole-wheat pizza dough (store-bought or homemade)
- 2 large eggs   1 ripe avocado, sliced
- 1/2 cup cherry tomatoes, halved   1/4 cup red onion, thinly sliced
- 1/4 cup feta cheese, crumbled   2 tablespoons olive oil
- Salt and pepper, to taste   Red pepper flakes (optional)
- Fresh arugula or baby spinach for topping

Instructions

1. Preheat your oven to 425°F (220°C). If you have a pizza stone, place it in the oven to preheat as well.

2. Roll out the whole-wheat pizza dough to your desired thickness on a piece of parchment paper.

3. Brush the top of the dough with 1 tablespoon of olive oil.

4. Carefully transfer the dough (with parchment paper) onto the preheated pizza stone or a baking sheet.

5. Bake the dough for about 8-10 minutes until it starts to turn golden brown.

6. Remove the pizza crust from the oven. Crack the eggs onto the pizza, and arrange the avocado slices, cherry tomatoes, and red onion around the eggs.

7. Return the pizza to the oven and bake for an additional 7-10 minutes, or until the egg whites are set and the yolks are cooked to your preference.

8. Sprinkle the crumbled feta cheese over the pizza.

9. Drizzle the remaining olive oil, and season with salt, pepper, and red pepper flakes (if using).

10. Add a handful of fresh arugula or baby spinach on top just before serving.

11. Slice and serve immediately.

Estimated Nutritional Value (per serving):

Calories: Approximately 350-400, Protein: 12-15g, Carbohydrates: 35-40g, Fat: 18-22g

If you prefer a crispy crust, pre-bake the dough a little longer before adding toppings.

Customize your pizza with additional toppings like sautéed spinach, mushrooms, or bell peppers.

For a vegan version, use a vegan cheese substitute and omit the eggs or use a plant-based egg alternative.

Quinoa-Oatmeal Cereal

Ingredients

- 1/2 cup quinoa, rinsed and drained   1/2 cup rolled oats
- 2 cups coconut milk (can use light coconut milk for a less rich version)
- 2 tablespoons maple syrup, plus more for serving
- 1/2 teaspoon ground cinnamon   1/4 teaspoon salt
- Fresh fruit for topping (such as berries, banana slices, or apple chunks)
- Optional add-ins: Chia seeds, flaxseeds, or nuts

Instructions

1. In a medium saucepan, combine the quinoa, rolled oats, coconut milk, maple syrup, cinnamon, and salt.

2. Bring the mixture to a boil over medium-high heat, then reduce the heat to low and simmer, stirring occasionally, for about 15-20 minutes or until the quinoa and oats are cooked and have absorbed most of the liquid.

3. Once cooked, remove the saucepan from the heat and let it sit covered for 5 minutes. The cereal will thicken upon standing.

4. Serve the quinoa-oatmeal cereal in bowls, topped with fresh fruit and additional maple syrup if desired. Sprinkle with chia seeds, flaxseeds, or nuts for added nutrition and texture.

Estimated Nutritional Value (per serving):

Calories: Approximately 250-300, Protein: 6-8g, Carbohydrates: 40-45g, Fat: 8-10g

To add more protein, stir in a scoop of your favorite protein powder or Greek yogurt.

The cereal can be made in advance and reheated throughout the week for quick breakfasts.

Adjust the sweetness by increasing or decreasing the amount of maple syrup according to your taste.

Blueberry-Ginger Smoothie

Ingredients

- 1 cup fresh or frozen blueberries
- 1 banana, sliced
- 1/2 inch piece of fresh ginger, peeled and grated
- 1/2 cup plain Greek yogurt
- 1 cup coconut milk (can use light coconut milk for a lighter version)
- 1 tablespoon honey or maple syrup (adjust to taste)
- A pinch of ground cinnamon (optional)
- Ice cubes (optional, use if you prefer a colder smoothie)

Instructions

1. In a blender, combine the blueberries, banana, grated ginger, Greek yogurt, coconut milk, and honey or maple syrup.

2. Add a pinch of ground cinnamon if desired. If using ice cubes, add them as well.

3. Blend on high speed until smooth and creamy. If the smoothie is too thick, add a little more coconut milk or water to achieve your desired consistency.

4. Taste the smoothie and adjust the sweetness if needed by adding more honey or maple syrup.

5. Pour the smoothie into glasses and serve immediately.

Estimated Nutritional Value (per serving):

Calories: Approximately 200-250, Protein: 6-8g, Carbohydrates: 35-40g, Fat: 6-8g

If using frozen blueberries, there's no need to add ice unless you prefer an extra cold smoothie.

Adjust the amount of ginger to suit your taste; increase it for more spice or decrease it for a milder flavor.

For a vegan version, use a plant-based yogurt and ensure your sweetener is vegan-friendly.

APPETIZERS AND SALADS

Savory Breakfast Salad

Ingredients

- 2 cups baby spinach or mixed greens
- 1 medium sweet potato, peeled and diced
- 1/2 cup cooked quinoa or farro
- 1/2 cup blueberries
- 1 avocado, sliced
- 2 tablespoons olive oil
- Salt and pepper to taste
- Optional: nuts or seeds for garnish (such as pumpkin seeds or sliced almonds)

1/4 cup hummus

1/4 cup cherry tomatoes, halved

2 eggs (hard-boiled or poached)

1 tablespoon balsamic vinegar

Instructions

1. Preheat the oven to 400°F (200°C). Toss the diced sweet potato in 1 tablespoon of olive oil, salt, and pepper. Spread on a baking sheet and roast for 20-25 minutes, or until tender and golden.

2. In a large bowl, combine the baby spinach or mixed greens with cooked quinoa or farro.

3. Add the roasted sweet potato, blueberries, cherry tomatoes, and sliced avocado to the bowl.

4. Top the salad with hummus and place the hard-boiled or poached eggs on top.

5. In a small bowl, whisk together the remaining olive oil and balsamic vinegar to create a dressing. Drizzle over the salad.

6. Season with salt and pepper to taste and garnish with nuts or seeds if desired.

7. Toss gently to combine and serve immediately.

Estimated Nutritional Value (per serving):

Calories: Approximately 350-400, Protein: 10-15g, Carbohydrates: 35-40g, Fat: 18-22g

For a vegan option, omit the eggs and add extra hummus or a plant-based protein like tofu.

The salad is versatile; feel free to add other vegetables or fruits as per your preference.

Store any leftover ingredients separately to keep the salad fresh for assembling later.

Greek Bruschetta

Ingredients

- 1 baguette, sliced into 1/2-inch thick rounds
- 1 cup cherry tomatoes, diced
- 1/4 cup red onion, finely chopped
- Fresh basil leaves, chopped (optional)
- 1/2 cup hummus or tzatziki sauce (for topping)

2 tablespoons olive oil

1/2 cucumber, diced

1/2 cup feta cheese, crumbled

Salt and pepper, to taste

Instructions

1. Preheat your oven to 375°F (190°C). Arrange the baguette slices on a baking sheet.

2. Brush each slice lightly with olive oil. Toast in the oven for about 5-7 minutes, or until the bread is golden and crisp.

3. In a mixing bowl, combine the diced cherry tomatoes, cucumber, red onion, and crumbled feta cheese. Add chopped basil if desired. Season with salt and pepper, and mix gently.

4. Once the bread is toasted, allow it to cool slightly. Spread a thin layer of hummus or tzatziki sauce on each slice, if using.

5. Top each slice of bread with the tomato, cucumber, and feta mixture.

6. Serve immediately, garnished with additional basil leaves if desired.

Estimated Nutritional Value (per serving):

Calories: Approximately 100-150 (varies based on the size of the bread and toppings), Protein: 3-5g, Carbohydrates: 15-20g, Fat: 5-7g

For a gluten-free version, use gluten-free bread or serve the tomato and cucumber mixture with gluten-free crackers.

Experiment with additional toppings like olives, roasted red peppers, or artichokes.

The tomato and cucumber mixture can be made ahead of time and stored in the refrigerator to enhance the flavors.

Authentic Greek Salad

Ingredients

- 3 medium ripe tomatoes, cut into wedges
- 1 small red onion, thinly sliced
- 1/2 cup Kalamata olives
- 200 grams (about 7 ounces) of feta cheese, sliced or crumbled
- 1/4 cup extra virgin olive oil
- 1 teaspoon dried oregano
- Fresh parsley, chopped (optional)

1 cucumber, sliced into half-moons

1 green bell pepper, sliced

2 tablespoons red wine vinegar

Salt and pepper to taste

Instructions

1. In a large salad bowl, combine the tomato wedges, cucumber slices, red onion, and green bell pepper.
2. Add the Kalamata olives to the bowl.
3. Place the feta cheese on top of the salad. If you prefer, you can crumble the feta over the salad instead of slicing it.
4. In a small bowl or jar, whisk together the extra virgin olive oil, red wine vinegar, dried oregano, salt, and pepper to create the dressing.
5. Drizzle the dressing over the salad just before serving.
6. Gently toss the salad to mix the ingredients without breaking the feta cheese too much.
7. Garnish with chopped fresh parsley if desired.
8. Serve immediately.

Estimated Nutritional Value (per serving):

Calories: Approximately 200-250, Protein: 6-8g, Carbohydrates: 10-12g, Fat: 18-20g

For the best flavor, use ripe, in-season tomatoes and high-quality extra virgin olive oil.

This salad is traditionally served with large pieces of vegetables and cheese, not chopped or minced.

The salad can be prepared a few hours in advance, but add the dressing just before serving to keep the vegetables crisp.

Lebanese Fattoush Salad

Ingredients

- 2 medium pita breads
- 2 medium tomatoes, diced
- 1 small red onion, thinly sliced
- 1/2 cup fresh parsley, chopped
- 1/2 cup sumac

4 cups romaine lettuce, chopped

1 cucumber, diced

1/2 cup radishes, thinly sliced

1/4 cup fresh mint, chopped

For the dressing

- 1/4 cup extra virgin olive oil
- 1 garlic clove, minced
- Salt and pepper to taste

2 tablespoons fresh lemon juice

1 teaspoon sumac

Instructions

1. Preheat the oven to 350°F (175°C). Split the pita breads into two rounds each and brush lightly with olive oil. Cut into bite-sized pieces and spread on a baking sheet. Bake until crisp and golden, about 10-15 minutes. Set aside to cool.

2. In a large salad bowl, combine the chopped romaine lettuce, tomatoes, cucumber, red onion, radishes, parsley, and mint. Toss gently to mix.

3. To make the dressing, whisk together the olive oil, lemon juice, minced garlic, sumac, salt, and pepper in a small bowl.

4. Drizzle the dressing over the salad and toss to evenly coat.

5. Just before serving, add the toasted pita chips to the salad and toss gently. Sprinkle additional sumac on top for added flavor.

6. Serve the Fattoush Salad immediately to ensure the pita chips stay crisp.

Estimated Nutritional Value (per serving):

Calories: Approximately 180-220, Protein: 3-4g, Carbohydrates: 20-25g, Fat: 10-12g

For a gluten-free version, use gluten-free pita bread or omit the pita chips.

The dressing can be made ahead and stored in the refrigerator. Dress the salad just before serving to keep it fresh.

Experiment with additional vegetables like bell peppers or grilled eggplant for more variety.

Cucumber Yogurt Salad with Fresh Mint, Lemon, and Olive Oil

Ingredients

- 2 large cucumbers, peeled and thinly sliced
- 1/4 cup fresh mint leaves, finely chopped
- 1 lemon, juiced and zested
- Salt and pepper to taste

2 cups plain Greek yogurt

2 tablespoons olive oil

1 garlic clove, minced

Optional: a pinch of ground cumin or dill

Instructions

1. In a large mixing bowl, combine the sliced cucumbers and Greek yogurt. Stir gently to mix.
2. Add the finely chopped mint leaves to the bowl.
3. In a small bowl, whisk together the olive oil, lemon juice, lemon zest, and minced garlic. Add a pinch of ground cumin or dill if desired.
4. Pour the olive oil mixture over the cucumber and yogurt. Stir to combine all the ingredients thoroughly.
5. Season the salad with salt and pepper to taste.
6. Refrigerate the salad for at least 30 minutes to allow the flavors to meld together.
7. Serve chilled, garnished with additional mint leaves or lemon zest.
8. Type of Cuisine: Mediterranean (Greek-Inspired)

Estimated Nutritional Value (per serving):

Calories: Approximately 100-150, Protein: 6-8g, Carbohydrates: 10-12g, Fat: 5-7g

For a vegan version, use a plant-based yogurt alternative.

If you prefer a thinner consistency, you can add a little water or more lemon juice to the yogurt.

The salad can be stored in the refrigerator for up to 2 days; however, it's best enjoyed fresh due to the cucumbers releasing water over time.

Herb-Roasted Olives & Tomatoes

Ingredients

- 2 cups mixed olives (such as Kalamata, green, and black)
- 1 cup cherry tomatoes
- 2 cloves garlic, thinly sliced
- 1 tablespoon fresh thyme, chopped
- Crushed red pepper flakes to taste
- Crusty bread or assorted cheeses for serving

- 3 tablespoons extra virgin olive oil
- 1 tablespoon fresh rosemary, chopped
- Zest of 1 lemon
- Salt and pepper to taste

Instructions

1. Preheat the oven to 375°F (190°C).
2. In a mixing bowl, combine the olives and cherry tomatoes.
3. Add the olive oil, garlic, rosemary, thyme, lemon zest, and red pepper flakes to the bowl. Season with salt and pepper. Toss to coat the olives and tomatoes evenly.
4. Spread the olive and tomato mixture in a single layer on a baking sheet.
5. Roast in the preheated oven for 20-25 minutes, or until the tomatoes are soft and the olives are fragrant.
6. Remove from the oven and let cool slightly.
7. Transfer to a serving dish, and serve warm with crusty bread or a selection of cheeses.

Estimated Nutritional Value (per serving):

Calories: Approximately 150-200, Protein: 1-2g, Carbohydrates: 5-10g, Fat: 15-20g

You can use any combination of olives based on your preference.

Adjust the amount of red pepper flakes based on your desired level of spiciness.

The herbs can be varied according to availability; dried herbs can be used in place of fresh, but in smaller quantities.

Mediterranean Nachos

Ingredients

- 4 large whole wheat pita bread rounds, cut into triangles
- 1 cup mixed olives (Kalamata, green, and black), chopped
- 1/2 cup sun-dried tomatoes, chopped   1 cup crumbled feta cheese
- 1/2 cup diced red onion   1/2 cup diced cucumber
- 1/2 cup diced red bell pepper   1/4 cup chopped fresh parsley
- 1/4 cup extra virgin olive oil   2 tablespoons red wine vinegar
- 1 teaspoon dried oregano   Salt and pepper to taste
- Optional toppings: Tzatziki sauce, hummus, or tahini

Instructions

1. Preheat your oven to 375°F (190°C).

2. Arrange the whole wheat pita triangles in a single layer on a baking sheet. Bake for about 10 minutes, or until the pita triangles are crispy and lightly browned. Remove from the oven and set aside to cool.

3. In a mixing bowl, combine the chopped olives and sun-dried tomatoes.

4. In a separate small bowl, whisk together the extra virgin olive oil, red wine vinegar, dried oregano, salt, and pepper to create the dressing.

5. Drizzle the dressing over the olive and sun-dried tomato mixture and toss to coat.

6. To assemble the nachos, spread the crispy pita triangles on a serving platter.

7. Sprinkle the crumbled feta cheese over the pita triangles.

8. Top with the dressed olive and sun-dried tomato mixture.

9. Add the diced red onion, cucumber, and red bell pepper on top.

10. Garnish with chopped fresh parsley.

11. Optionally, drizzle with Tzatziki sauce, hummus, or tahini for extra flavor.

12. Serve the Mediterranean Nachos immediately.

Estimated Nutritional Value (per serving):

Calories: Approximately 300-350, Protein: 8-10g, Carbohydrates: 30-35g, Fat: 18-20g

Customize the toppings to your liking; you can add chopped artichoke hearts, roasted red peppers, or thinly sliced red chili peppers for extra spice.

Ensure the pita triangles are crispy to provide a sturdy base for the nachos.

If you prefer warm nachos, you can briefly heat them in the oven after assembling.

Mezze Platter

Ingredients

- 1 cup roasted red pepper dip (store-bought or homemade)
- 1 cucumber, sliced into rounds
- 2 carrots, peeled and sliced into sticks
- 1 cup marinated olives (Kalamata, green, or mixed)
- 1 cup crumbled feta cheese
- 1/2 cup fresh figs, halved
- 1 cup pita chips or crackers
- Fresh herbs for garnish (such as mint or parsley)

Instructions

1. Arrange a large platter or serving board.
2. Place the roasted red pepper dip in a small bowl and position it at one end of the platter.
3. Arrange the cucumber slices and carrot sticks in a neat row on one side of the platter.
4. Place the marinated olives in a small bowl or spread them out on the platter.
5. Scatter the crumbled feta cheese over the platter.
6. Arrange the fresh figs among the other components.
7. Fill the remaining space with pita chips or crackers.
8. Garnish the platter with fresh herbs for a pop of color.
9. Serve the mezze platter as a delightful and shareable appetizer.

Mediterranean Appetizer Pinwheels

Ingredients

- 1 sheet puff pastry (thawed if frozen)   1/2 cup crumbled feta cheese
- 1/4 cup Kalamata olives, finely chopped
- 1/4 cup roasted red peppers, finely chopped
- 1/4 cup Swiss cheese, grated   1/4 teaspoon dried oregano
- 1/4 teaspoon garlic powder   1 egg (for egg wash)
- Fresh parsley or basil leaves for garnish (optional)

Instructions

1. Preheat your oven to 375°F (190°C). Line a baking sheet with parchment paper.
2. Roll out the puff pastry sheet on a lightly floured surface into a rectangle.
3. In a bowl, combine the crumbled feta cheese, chopped Kalamata olives, roasted red peppers, Swiss cheese, dried oregano, and garlic powder. Mix well.
4. Spread the Mediterranean cheese and olive mixture evenly over the puff pastry sheet, leaving a small border along the edges.
5. Starting from one long side, tightly roll up the pastry sheet into a log, like a jelly roll.
6. Slice the log into 1-inch thick pinwheels and place them on the prepared baking sheet.
7. In a small bowl, beat the egg to create an egg wash. Brush the pinwheels with the egg wash for a golden finish.
8. Bake in the preheated oven for 15-20 minutes or until the pinwheels are puffed and golden.
9. Remove from the oven and let cool for a few minutes.

10. Garnish with fresh parsley or basil leaves if desired.

11. Serve the Mediterranean Appetizer Pinwheels warm or at room temperature.

Estimated Nutritional Value (per serving):

Calories: Approximately 90-120 per pinwheel (varies based on size and ingredients), Protein: 2-3g per pinwheel, Carbohydrates: 5-7g per pinwheel, Fat: 7-9g per pinwheel

You can customize the filling with additional ingredients like sun-dried tomatoes, fresh herbs, or spinach.

Ensure the puff pastry is thawed but still cold for easier handling.

Experiment with different cheeses for variety.

White Bean Artichoke Dip

Ingredients

- 1 can (15 ounces) cannellini or white beans, drained and rinsed
- 1 can (14 ounces) artichoke hearts, drained and roughly chopped
- 1/4 cup grated Parmesan cheese   1/4 cup mayonnaise
- 1/4 cup sour cream or Greek yogurt   2 cloves garlic, minced
- 1 tablespoon lemon juice   1 teaspoon dried basil
- 1 teaspoon dried oregano   Salt and pepper to taste
- 1/4 cup chopped fresh parsley (for garnish)
- Pita chips, carrot sticks, cucumber slices, or bell pepper strips for dipping

Instructions

1. In a food processor, combine the drained white beans, chopped artichoke hearts, grated Parmesan cheese, mayonnaise, sour cream or Greek yogurt, minced garlic, lemon juice, dried basil, and dried oregano.

2. Process the mixture until smooth and creamy. If it's too thick, you can add a splash of water or olive oil to reach your desired consistency.

3. Taste the dip and season with salt and pepper to your liking. Blend again to incorporate the seasoning.

4. Transfer the white bean artichoke dip to a serving bowl.

5. Garnish with chopped fresh parsley.

6. Serve the dip with pita chips, carrot sticks, cucumber slices, or bell pepper strips for dipping.

Estimated Nutritional Value (per serving, excluding dippers):

Calories: Approximately 90-120 (varies based on portion size), Protein: 3-4g, Carbohydrates: 6-8g, Fat: 6-8g

You can adjust the garlic and lemon juice to suit your taste preferences.

This dip can be made ahead and stored in the refrigerator for a day or two; it often tastes even better after flavors meld.

Consider adding a pinch of red pepper flakes for a hint of spice.

CHAPTER FOUR

SOUPS AND STEWS

Zucchini Basil Soup with Lemon

Ingredients

- 4 medium zucchinis, chopped
- 2 cloves garlic, minced
- 1 cup fresh basil leaves
- Salt and pepper to taste

1 onion, chopped

4 cups vegetable broth

1 lemon, juiced and zested

Olive oil for drizzling

Instructions

1. In a large pot, sauté onions and garlic in olive oil until translucent.
2. Add zucchinis and cook for 5 minutes.
3. Pour in vegetable broth, bring to a boil, and simmer for 15 minutes.
4. Add basil leaves, lemon juice, and zest. Blend until smooth.
5. Season with salt and pepper. Serve hot, garnished with basil leaves and a drizzle of olive oil.

Estimated Nutritional Value: Per serving - Calories: 120, Carbohydrates: 15g, Protein: 3g, Fat: 6g Serving Ideas: Garnish with fresh basil leaves and a drizzle of olive oil. Serve with crusty bread.

French Lentil and Carrot Soup

Instructions

- Ingredients (Serves 6):   1 cup French lentils, rinsed and drained
- 4 carrots, diced   1 onion, chopped
- 3 cloves garlic, minced   6 cups vegetable broth
- 1 tsp dried thyme   Salt and pepper to taste
- Greek yogurt and fresh parsley for garnish

Instructions

1. In a large pot, sauté onions and garlic in olive oil until fragrant.
2. Add lentils, carrots, vegetable broth, and thyme. Bring to a boil, then reduce heat and simmer for 30 minutes.
3. Use an immersion blender to partially blend the soup, leaving some texture.
4. Season with salt and pepper. Serve hot, garnished with a dollop of Greek yogurt and fresh parsley.

Estimated Nutritional Value: Per serving - Calories: 220, Carbohydrates: 40g, Protein: 12g, Fat: 1g Serving Ideas: Top with a dollop of Greek yogurt and sprinkle with fresh parsley. Serve with a slice of crusty bread.

Slow-Cooker Minestrone

Ingredients

- 2 cups diced tomatoes (canned or fresh)   1 cup diced carrots
- 1 cup diced celery   1 cup diced zucchini
- 1 onion, chopped   3 cloves garlic, minced
- 4 cups vegetable broth
- 1 cup cooked pasta (e.g., small shells or ditalini)
- 1 tsp dried basil   Salt and pepper to taste
- Grated Parmesan cheese and garlic bread for serving

Instructions

1. Place all ingredients (except pasta) in a slow cooker. Cook on low for 6-8 hours or until vegetables are tender.
2. About 30 minutes before serving, stir in the cooked pasta.
3. Season with salt and pepper. Serve hot, sprinkled with grated Parmesan cheese, and accompanied by garlic bread.

Estimated Nutritional Value: Per serving - Calories: 180, Carbohydrates: 35g, Protein: 8g, Fat: 1g Serving Ideas: Sprinkle with grated Parmesan cheese and serve with garlic bread.

Mediterranean Chicken Orzo Soup

Ingredients

- 1 lb. boneless, skinless chicken thighs, cut into bite-sized pieces
- 1 cup orzo pasta — 1 onion, chopped
- 3 cloves garlic, minced — 4 cups chicken broth
- 1 lemon, juiced and zested — 1 tsp dried oregano
- Salt and pepper to taste — Fresh dill and lemon slices for garnish

Instructions

1. In a large pot, sauté onions and garlic in olive oil until translucent.
2. Add chicken pieces and cook until browned.
3. Stir in orzo, chicken broth, lemon juice, and zest. Simmer for 15 minutes.
4. Season with dried oregano, salt, and pepper. Serve hot, garnished with fresh dill and lemon slices.

Estimated Nutritional Value: Per serving - Calories: 280, Carbohydrates: 35g, Protein: 20g, Fat: 7g Serving Ideas: Top with fresh dill and serve with a slice of lemon.

Ingredients

- 10 garlic cloves, peeled and sliced
- 4 slices of stale bread, cubed
- 4 tbsp. olive oil

4 cups vegetable broth

4 eggs

Salt and pepper to taste

Instructions

1. In a saucepan, heat olive oil and sauté garlic slices until fragrant.
2. Add vegetable broth and bring to a simmer. Cook for 10 minutes.
3. Toast the bread cubes in a separate pan until golden brown.
4. Poach eggs in the soup until desired doneness.
5. Serve hot, placing a poached egg on top of each bowl and garnishing with crispy croutons.

Estimated Nutritional Value: Per serving - Calories: 180, Carbohydrates: 25g, Protein: 5g, Fat: 7g Serving Ideas: Serve with a poached egg on top and crispy croutons.

Moroccan Harira (Lentil and Chickpea Soup)

Ingredients

- 1 cup dried green lentils, rinsed and drained
- 1 cup cooked chickpeas
- 3 cloves garlic, minced
- 1/2 cup chopped cilantro
- 1/2 tsp ground cumin
- 1/2 tsp paprika
- Lemon wedges and flatbread for serving

1 onion, chopped

2 tomatoes, diced

1/4 cup chopped parsley

1/2 tsp ground coriander

Salt and pepper to taste

Instructions

1. In a large pot, sauté onions and garlic in olive oil until translucent.

2. Add lentils, chickpeas, tomatoes, and spices. Cook for 10 minutes.

3. Stir in cilantro and parsley. Simmer for an additional 10 minutes.

4. Season with salt and pepper. Serve hot, garnished with fresh cilantro and lemon wedges. Accompany with warm flatbread.

Moroccan Estimated Nutritional Value: Per serving - Calories: 280, Carbohydrates: 45g, Protein: 15g, Fat: 4g
Serving Ideas: Garnish with fresh cilantro and lemon wedges. Serve with flatbread.

Mediterranean Roasted Potatoes Nachos

Ingredients

- 4 medium potatoes, sliced into rounds
- 1/2 cup black olives, sliced
- 1/4 cup fresh parsley, chopped
- Olive oil for drizzling

1 cup shredded mozzarella cheese

1/4 cup red onion, finely chopped

1 tsp dried oregano

Salt and pepper to taste

Instructions

1. Preheat the oven to 400°F (200°C).

2. Place potato rounds on a baking sheet, drizzle with olive oil, and season with salt and pepper. Roast for 20-25 minutes until golden and crispy.

3. Remove from the oven and sprinkle with mozzarella cheese, black olives, and red onion.

4. Return to the oven and bake for an additional 5-7 minutes until the cheese is melted and bubbly.

Sprinkle with dried oregano and fresh parsley. Serve hot. Estimated Nutritional Value: Per serving - Calories: 250, Carbohydrates: 30g, Protein: 6g, Fat: 12g Serving Ideas: Top with Greek yogurt, diced tomatoes, and fresh parsley. Serve as an appetizer or a unique snack.

Youvarlakia (Greek Meatball Soup)

Ingredients

- 1 lb ground beef or lamb   1/2 cup rice
- 1 onion, finely chopped   2 cloves garlic, minced
- 2 eggs   1/4 cup fresh parsley, chopped
- 6 cups chicken broth   Juice of 1 lemon
- Salt and pepper to taste   Lemon wedges and crusty bread for serving

Instructions

1. In a bowl, combine ground meat, rice, onion, garlic, eggs, and parsley. Form into small meatballs.
2. In a large pot, bring chicken broth to a boil. Add meatballs and simmer for 20-25 minutes until meatballs are cooked through.
3. Season with lemon juice, salt, and pepper. Serve hot, garnished with a lemon wedge and accompanied by crusty bread.

Greek Estimated Nutritional Value: Per serving - Calories: 280, Carbohydrates: 15g, Protein: 18g, Fat: 15g Serving Ideas: Garnish with a lemon wedge and serve with crusty bread.

Tomato Basil Soup

Ingredients

- 4 cups canned crushed tomatoes
- 2 cloves garlic, minced
- 2 cups vegetable broth
- Salt and pepper to taste
- Fresh basil and Parmesan cheese for garnish

1 onion, chopped

1/4 cup fresh basil leaves, chopped

2 tbsp. olive oil

Instructions

1. In a large pot, sauté onions and garlic in olive oil until translucent.
2. Add crushed tomatoes, vegetable broth, and fresh basil. Simmer for 15-20 minutes.
3. Blend the soup until smooth using an immersion blender.
4. Season with salt and pepper. Serve hot, garnished with fresh basil leaves and Parmesan cheese.

Estimated Nutritional Value: Per serving - Calories: 150, Carbohydrates: 20g, Protein: 4g, Fat: 6g Serving Ideas: Top with fresh basil leaves and a sprinkle of Parmesan cheese. Serve with crusty bread.

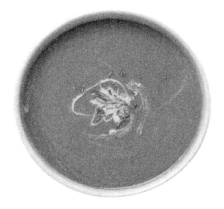

Easy Ratatouille (One Pot Vegetable Stew)

Ingredients

- 1 eggplant, diced
- 2 red bell peppers, diced
- 3 cloves garlic, minced
- 2 tsp dried thyme
- 2 tbsp. olive oil

2 zucchinis, diced

1 onion, chopped

2 cups diced tomatoes (canned or fresh)

2 tsp dried rosemary

Salt and pepper to taste

Instructions

1. In a large pot, sauté onions and garlic in olive oil until fragrant.
2. Add eggplant, zucchinis, and red bell peppers. Cook for 10 minutes.
3. Stir in diced tomatoes, thyme, and rosemary. Simmer for 15-20 minutes.
4. Season with salt and pepper. Serve hot as a side dish or over couscous or quinoa.

Estimated Nutritional Value: Per serving - Calories: 120, Carbohydrates: 20g, Protein: 3g, Fat: 4g Serving Ideas: Serve as a side dish or over couscous or quinoa.

Salmorejo (Spanish Chilled Tomato Soup)

Estimated Nutritional Value: Per serving - Calories: 160, Carbohydrates: 20g, Protein: 3g, Fat: 8g Serving Ideas: Garnish with hard-boiled egg slices and drizzle with olive oil. Serve chilled on a hot day.

Ingredients

- 6 ripe tomatoes, peeled and seeded
- 2 slices stale bread, soaked in water and squeezed dry
- 1/2 cup olive oil
- 2 tbsp. red wine vinegar
- Hard-boiled egg slices and extra olive oil for garnish

2 cloves garlic, minced

Salt and pepper to taste

Instructions

1. In a blender, combine tomatoes, soaked bread, olive oil, garlic, and red wine vinegar. Blend until smooth.

2. Season with salt and pepper. Chill in the refrigerator for at least 2 hours before serving.

3. Garnish with hard-boiled egg slices and a drizzle of olive oil. Serve chilled.

Estimated Nutritional Value: Per serving - Calories: 120, Carbohydrates: 20g, Protein: 3g, Fat: 4g Serving Ideas: Serve as a side dish or over couscous or quinoa.

Stracciatella Soup

Ingredients

- 4 cups chicken or vegetable broth
- 1/4 cup grated Parmesan cheese
- Salt and pepper to taste

2 eggs

2 tbsp fresh parsley, chopped

Instructions

1. In a pot, bring the broth to a gentle simmer.

2. In a bowl, beat the eggs and mix in grated Parmesan cheese.

3. Slowly pour the egg mixture into the simmering broth, stirring constantly to create delicate egg ribbons.

4. Season with salt and pepper. Garnish with fresh parsley. Serve hot.

Estimated Nutritional Value: Per serving - Calories: 150, Carbohydrates: 10g, Protein: 7g, Fat: 9g Serving Ideas: Top with grated Parmesan cheese and fresh parsley. Serve as an appetizer or a light meal.

Greek White Bean Soup with Orange Slices and Olive Oil

Ingredients

- 2 cups dried white beans, soaked overnight and drained
- 1 onion, chopped
- 1 bay leaf
- 1/4 cup olive oil
- Orange slices and olive oil for garnish
- Crusty bread for serving

3 cloves garlic, minced

2 oranges, peeled and sliced

Salt and pepper to taste

Instructions

1. In a large pot, sauté onions and garlic in olive oil until translucent.

2. Add soaked white beans, bay leaf, and enough water to cover. Simmer for 1-2 hours or until beans are tender.

3. Season with salt and pepper. Remove the bay leaf and discard.

4. Ladle the soup into bowls, garnish with orange slices, and drizzle with olive oil. Serve with crusty bread.

Estimated Nutritional Value: Per serving - Calories: 220, Carbohydrates: 35g, Protein: 10g, Fat: 6g Serving Ideas: Garnish with orange slices and a drizzle of olive oil. Serve with crusty bread.Zucchini Basil Soup with Lemon

Slow Cooker Beef Stew with Eggplant and Zucchini

Ingredients

- 2 lbs. beef stew meat, cut into cubes 1 eggplant, diced
- 2 zucchinis, diced   1 onion, chopped
- 3 cloves garlic, minced   2 cups diced tomatoes (canned or fresh)
- 1 cup beef broth   2 tsp dried oregano
- Salt and pepper to taste   Fresh herbs for garnish

Instructions

1. In a skillet, brown the beef cubes over medium-high heat. Transfer them to a slow cooker.

2. In the same skillet, sauté onions and garlic until translucent. Add diced tomatoes and beef broth, scraping up any browned bits from the bottom of the skillet.

3. Pour the tomato mixture over the beef in the slow cooker. Add diced eggplant, zucchinis, and dried oregano. Stir to combine.

4. Cover and cook on low for 6-8 hours or until the beef is tender.

5. Season with salt and pepper. Serve hot, garnished with fresh herbs, and over cooked couscous or rice.

Estimated Nutritional Value: Per serving - Calories: 350, Carbohydrates: 20g, Protein: 30g, Fat: 16g Serving Ideas: Serve over cooked couscous or rice, garnish with fresh herbs.

CHAPTER FIVE

MAIN COURSE

Mediterranean Stuffed Bell Peppers

Ingredients

- 4 large bell peppers, assorted colors
- 1 cup quinoa, cooked
- 1 can (15 oz.) chickpeas, drained and rinsed
- 1 cup cherry tomatoes, halved
- 1/2 cup Kalamata olives, pitted and chopped
- 1/4 cup feta cheese, crumbled
- 1/4 cup fresh parsley, chopped
- 2 cloves garlic, minced
- 2 tbsp. olive oil
- 1 tsp dried oregano
- Salt and pepper, to taste

Instructions

1. Preheat the oven to 375°F (190°C).
2. Cut the tops off the bell peppers and remove the seeds and membranes.
3. In a large bowl, combine cooked quinoa, chickpeas, cherry tomatoes, olives, feta cheese, parsley, garlic, olive oil, oregano, salt, and pepper.
4. Stuff the bell peppers with the quinoa mixture and place them in a baking dish.
5. Cover with foil and bake for 30 minutes. Uncover and bake for another 10-15 minutes, or until the peppers are tender.

6. Serve warm.

Estimated Nutritional Value (per serving):

Calories: 250, Protein: 9g, Carbohydrates: 35g, Fat: 10g, Fiber: 6g

Eggplant and Lentil Moussaka

Ingredients

- 2 large eggplants, sliced into 1/2 inch rounds
- 1 cup green lentils, cooked
- 2 cloves garlic, minced
- 1 tsp cinnamon
- 1/4 cup fresh parsley, chopped
- Salt and pepper, to taste

1 onion, finely chopped

1 can (14 oz.) crushed tomatoes

1/2 tsp nutmeg

Olive oil

For the béchamel sauce

- 2 tbsp. butter
- 2 cups milk
- Pinch of nutmeg

2 tbsp. flour

1/4 cup Parmesan cheese, grated

Instructions

1. Preheat the oven to 375°F (190°C).

2. Brush eggplant slices with olive oil and season with salt and pepper. Grill until tender.

3. In a skillet, sauté onions and garlic in olive oil until translucent. Add cooked lentils, crushed tomatoes, cinnamon, nutmeg, and parsley. Cook for 5 minutes.

4. For béchamel sauce, melt butter in a saucepan, whisk in flour until smooth. Gradually add milk, stirring continuously until thickened. Stir in Parmesan and a pinch of nutmeg.

5. In a baking dish, layer grilled eggplant, lentil mixture, and béchamel sauce. Repeat layers and top with béchamel sauce.

6. Bake for 40 minutes, or until golden brown.

Estimated Nutritional Value (per serving):

Calories: 320, Protein: 14g, Carbohydrates: 38g, Fat: 14g, Fiber: 9g, Sodium: 280mg

Roasted Vegetable and Quinoa Salad

Ingredients

- 1 cup quinoa, cooked
- 1 red bell pepper, chopped
- 1 red onion, sliced
- 1/4 cup feta cheese, crumbled
- 3 tbsp. olive oil
- Salt and pepper, to taste

- 1 zucchini, sliced
- 1 yellow bell pepper, chopped
- 1/2 cup cherry tomatoes, halved
- 1/4 cup fresh basil, chopped
- 2 tbsp balsamic vinegar

Instructions

1. Preheat the oven to 400°F (200°C).

2. Toss zucchini, bell peppers, and red onion with 2 tablespoons olive oil, salt, and pepper. Roast for 20-25 minutes.

3. In a large bowl, mix roasted vegetables with cooked quinoa, cherry tomatoes, feta cheese, and basil.

4. Drizzle with balsamic vinegar and the remaining olive oil. Toss gently.

5. Serve either warm or at room temperature.

Estimated Nutritional Value (per serving):

Calories: 280, Protein: 8g, Carbohydrates: 40g, Fat: 11g, Fiber: 5g

Mediterranean Vegetable Paella

Ingredients

- 1 cup Arborio rice
- 1 onion, finely chopped
- 1 yellow bell pepper, sliced
- 1 cup frozen peas
- 1 tsp smoked paprika
- 1/4 cup fresh parsley, chopped
- Salt and pepper, to taste

2 cups vegetable broth
1 red bell pepper, sliced
1 zucchini, diced
3 cloves garlic, minced
1/2 tsp saffron threads
2 tbsp. olive oil
Lemon wedges, for serving

Instructions

1. In a large skillet, heat olive oil over medium heat. Sauté onion and garlic until translucent.
2. Add bell peppers and zucchini, cooking until slightly soft.
3. Stir in Arborio rice, smoked paprika, saffron, salt, and pepper. Cook for 1 minute.
4. Add vegetable broth, bring to a boil, and then reduce heat to low. Cover and simmer for 20 minutes.
5. Add peas and cook for an additional 5 minutes.
6. Remove from heat, let it sit covered for 10 minutes.
7. Garnish with parsley and serve with lemon wedges.

Estimated Nutritional Value (per serving):

Calories: 310, Protein: 7g, Carbohydrates: 55g, Fat: 7g, Fiber: 4g

Chickpea and Spinach Stew

Ingredients

- 2 cans (15 oz. each) chickpeas, drained and rinsed
- 4 cups fresh spinach
- 2 cloves garlic, minced
- 1 tsp cumin
- 1/2 tsp coriander
- Salt and pepper, to taste

1 onion, chopped

1 can (14 oz.) diced tomatoes

1 tsp paprika

2 tbsp. olive oil

1/4 cup fresh cilantro, chopped

Instructions

1. In a large pot, heat olive oil over medium heat. Sauté onion and garlic until soft.
2. Add cumin, paprika, and coriander, cooking for 1 minute.
3. Stir in chickpeas and diced tomatoes. Simmer for 10 minutes.
4. Add spinach, cook until wilted.
5. Season with salt and pepper, and garnish with cilantro.
6. Serve hot.

Estimated Nutritional Value (per serving):

Calories: 280, Protein: 14g, Carbohydrates: 45g, Fat: 8g, Fiber: 12g

Mediterranean Vegetable Tart

Ingredients

- 1 pre-made pie crust
- 1 zucchini, thinly sliced
- 1 red bell pepper, thinly sliced
- 2 tbsp. olive oil
- Salt and pepper, to taste

1 cup ricotta cheese

1 yellow squash, thinly sliced

1 eggplant, thinly sliced

1 tsp thyme

1/4 cup grated Parmesan cheese

Instructions

1. Preheat the oven to 375°F (190°C).
2. Spread ricotta evenly over the pie crust.
3. Arrange zucchini, squash, bell pepper, and eggplant slices over the ricotta in a circular pattern.
4. Drizzle with olive oil, sprinkle thyme, salt, and pepper.
5. Bake for 35-40 minutes until vegetables are tender and crust is golden.
6. Sprinkle with Parmesan cheese and serve warm.

Estimated Nutritional Value (per serving):

Calories: 270, Protein: 9g, Carbohydrates: 28g, Fat: 14g, Fiber: 3g

Mediterranean Lentil Soup

Ingredients

- 1 cup green lentils, rinsed
- 2 carrots, diced
- 3 cloves garlic, minced
- 4 cups vegetable broth

1 onion, chopped

2 celery stalks, diced

1 can (14 oz.) diced tomatoes

1 tsp cumin

- 1/2 tsp thyme
- Salt and pepper, to taste

2 tbsp. olive oil

1/4 cup fresh parsley, chopped

Instructions

1. In a large pot, heat olive oil over medium heat. Sauté onion, carrots, and celery until soft.
2. Add garlic, cumin, and thyme, cooking for 1 minute.
3. Stir in lentils, diced tomatoes, and vegetable broth. Bring to a boil.
4. Reduce heat, cover, and simmer for 30 minutes or until lentils are tender.
5. Season with salt and pepper.
6. Garnish with parsley and serve hot.

Estimated Nutritional Value (per serving):

Calories: 220, Protein: 12g, Carbohydrates: 33g, Fat: 5g, Fiber: 10g

Roasted Red Pepper and Tomato Pasta

Ingredients

- 12 oz. whole wheat pasta
- 1 can (14 oz.) diced tomatoes
- 3 cloves garlic, minced
- 2 tbsp. olive oil
- Salt and pepper, to taste

2 red bell peppers, roasted and chopped

1 onion, chopped

1/4 cup fresh basil, chopped

1/4 tsp red pepper flakes

Grated Parmesan cheese, for serving

Instructions

1. Cook pasta according to package instructions; drain.
2. In a skillet, heat olive oil over medium heat. Sauté onion and garlic until soft.

3. Add roasted red peppers, diced tomatoes, and red pepper flakes. Simmer for 10 minutes.

4. Toss the sauce with the cooked pasta and basil.

5. Season with salt and pepper.

6. Serve with grated Parmesan cheese.

Estimated Nutritional Value (per serving):

Calories: 350, Protein: 12g, Carbohydrates: 60g, Fat: 9g, Fiber: 10g

Mediterranean Farro Salad

Ingredients

- 1 cup farro, cooked
- 1 red onion, finely chopped
- 1/2 cup sun-dried tomatoes, chopped
- 1/4 cup fresh mint, chopped
- 2 tbsp. lemon juice

- 1 cucumber, diced
- 1/2 cup Kalamata olives, pitted and sliced
- 1/4 cup feta cheese, crumbled
- 3 tbsp. olive oil
- Salt and pepper, to taste

Instructions

1. In a large bowl, combine cooked farro, cucumber, red onion, olives, sun-dried tomatoes, feta cheese, and mint.

2. In a small bowl, whisk together olive oil and lemon juice. Pour over the salad.

3. Toss gently to combine.

4. Season with salt and pepper.

5. Serve chilled or at room temperature.

Estimated Nutritional Value (per serving):

Calories: 270, Protein: 8g, Carbohydrates: 40g, Fat: 10g, Fiber: 6g

CHAPTER SIX

DESSERTS

Greek Lemon Roasted Potatoes

Ingredients

- 2 lbs. small potatoes, halved
- Juice of 2 lemons
- 1 tbsp. dried oregano
- Fresh parsley, chopped, for garnish

1/4 cup olive oil

3 cloves garlic, minced

Salt and pepper, to taste

Instructions

1. Preheat the oven to 400°F (200°C).
2. In a large bowl, toss potatoes with olive oil, lemon juice, garlic, oregano, salt, and pepper.
3. Spread potatoes in a single layer on a baking sheet.
4. Roast for 45-50 minutes, or until golden and crisp.
5. Garnish with fresh parsley before serving.

Estimated Nutritional Value (per serving):

Calories: 220, Protein: 4g, Carbohydrates: 38g, Fat: 7g, Fiber: 5g

Greek Yogurt with Honey and Walnuts

Ingredients

- 2 cups Greek yogurt
- 1/2 cup walnuts, chopped

4 tbsp. honey

1/4 tsp cinnamon

Instructions

1. Divide the Greek yogurt into four bowls.

2. Drizzle each bowl of yogurt with 1 tablespoon of honey.

3. Sprinkle chopped walnuts and a pinch of cinnamon over the top.

4. Serve chilled.

Estimated Nutritional Value (per serving):

Calories: 200, Protein: 12g, Carbohydrates: 18g, Fat: 9g, Fiber: 1g

Fig and Almond Cake

Ingredients

- 1 cup dried figs, chopped
- 1/2 cup honey
- 1 tsp baking powder
- Zest of 1 orange
- 2 cups almond flour
- 3 eggs
- 1 tsp vanilla extract

Instructions

1. Preheat the oven to 350°F (175°C). Grease a 9-inch cake pan.

2. In a bowl, mix almond flour and baking powder.

3. In another bowl, beat eggs, honey, vanilla extract, and orange zest until well combined.

4. Gradually add the dry ingredients to the wet ingredients, stirring until just combined.

5. Fold in the chopped figs.

6. Pour the batter into the prepared pan and bake for 25-30 minutes.

7. Let cool before serving.

Estimated Nutritional Value (per serving):

Calories: 280, Protein: 8g, Carbohydrates: 35g, Fat: 14g, Fiber: 4g

Baklava

Ingredients

- 1 package phyllo dough, thawed
- 1 cup butter, melted

2 cups mixed nuts, finely chopped

1 tsp ground cinnamon

For the syrup

- 1 cup water
- 1/2 cup honey
- Zest of 1 lemon

1 cup sugar

1/2 tsp vanilla extract

Instructions

1. Preheat the oven to 350°F (175°C). Grease a 9x13 inch baking dish.
2. Mix chopped nuts with cinnamon. Set aside.
3. Place one sheet of phyllo in the baking dish, brush with melted butter. Repeat with half of the phyllo sheets.
4. Spread the nut mixture over the phyllo. Layer the remaining phyllo sheets, brushing each with butter.
5. Cut the baklava into diamond shapes and bake for 50 minutes.
6. For the syrup, combine water, sugar, honey, vanilla extract, and lemon zest in a saucepan. Bring to a boil, then simmer for 10 minutes.
7. Pour the syrup over the hot baklava.
8. Let cool before serving.

Estimated Nutritional Value (per serving):

Calories: 330, Protein: 5g, Carbohydrates: 40g, Fat: 18g, Fiber: 2g

Orange and Almond Cake

Ingredients

- 2 oranges, boiled and pureed
- 1 cup sugar
- 1 tsp baking powder

3 cups almond flour

6 eggs

Instructions

1. Preheat the oven to 375°F (190°C). Grease a 9-inch cake pan.
2. Beat eggs and sugar until fluffy.
3. Stir in the orange puree.
4. Fold in almond flour and baking powder.
5. Pour the batter into the pan and bake for 1 hour.
6. Let cool before serving.

Estimated Nutritional Value (per serving):

Calories: 300, Protein: 10g, Carbohydrates: 32g, Fat: 16g, Fiber: 4g

Lemon and Olive Oil Cake

Ingredients

- 1 3/4 cups all-purpose flour
- 1/2 cup olive oil
- Juice and zest of 2 lemons
- 1/2 tsp salt

1 cup sugar

3 eggs

2 tsp baking powder

Instructions

1. Preheat the oven to 350°F (175°C). Grease a 9-inch cake pan.
2. Beat eggs and sugar until light and fluffy.
3. Gradually mix in olive oil, lemon juice, and zest.

4. In a separate bowl, combine flour, baking powder, and salt.

5. Gently fold the dry ingredients into the wet mixture until just combined.

6. Pour the batter into the prepared pan and bake for 35-40 minutes, or until a toothpick inserted into the center comes out clean.

7. Let cool before serving.

Estimated Nutritional Value (per serving):

Calories: 310, Protein: 5g, Carbohydrates: 42g, Fat: 14g, Fiber: 1g

Mediterranean Rice Pudding

Ingredients

- 1 cup Arborio rice
- 1/3 cup sugar
- Zest of 1 lemon

  4 cups milk

  1 cinnamon stick

  1/2 tsp vanilla extract

Instructions

1. In a saucepan, combine rice, milk, sugar, and cinnamon stick. Bring to a low boil, then reduce heat to simmer.

2. Cook, stirring occasionally, until the rice is tender and the mixture has thickened (about 30-40 minutes).

3. Remove from heat and stir in lemon zest and vanilla extract.

4. Discard the cinnamon stick and let the pudding cool.

5. Serve chilled or at room temperature, garnished with a sprinkle of cinnamon.

Estimated Nutritional Value (per serving):

Calories: 200, Protein: 5g, Carbohydrates: 36g, Fat: 4g, Fiber: 1g

Almond and Honey Florentines

Ingredients

- 1 cup sliced almonds
- 2 tbsp butter
- Zest of 1 orange

1/3 cup honey

1/4 cup flour

Pinch of salt

Instructions

1. Preheat the oven to 350°F (175°C). Line a baking sheet with parchment paper.

2. In a saucepan, heat honey and butter until melted. Stir in flour, orange zest, and salt.

3. Mix in sliced almonds until well coated.

4. Drop teaspoonfuls of the mixture onto the baking sheet, spaced well apart.

5. Bake for 10-12 minutes, or until golden brown.

6. Let cool on the baking sheet before removing.

Estimated Nutritional Value (per serving):

Calories: 120, Protein: 2g, Carbohydrates: 14g, Fat: 7g, Fiber: 1g

Poached Pears in Red Wine

Ingredients

- 4 ripe pears, peeled and cored
- 1/2 cup sugar
- Peel of 1 orange

2 cups red wine

1 cinnamon stick

Instructions

- In a large saucepan, combine red wine, sugar, cinnamon stick, and orange peel. Bring to a simmer.

- Add pears and simmer gently for 15-20 minutes, or until tender.

- Remove pears and reduce the sauce over high heat until syrupy.

- Serve pears drizzled with the red wine syrup.

Estimated Nutritional Value (per serving):

Calories: 240, Protein: 1g, Carbohydrates: 50g, Fat: 0g, Fiber: 5g

Pistachio and Apricot Biscotti

Ingredients

- 2 cups all-purpose flour
- 1/2 cup pistachios, chopped
- 3 eggs
- 1 tsp vanilla extract

1 cup sugar

1/2 cup dried apricots, chopped

1 tsp baking powder

Instructions

1. Preheat the oven to 350°F (175°C). Line a baking sheet with parchment paper.

2. In a bowl, combine flour, sugar, baking powder, pistachios, and apricots.

3. In another bowl, beat eggs and vanilla. Add to the dry ingredients, mixing to form a dough.

4. Divide dough in half and shape into two logs on the baking sheet.

5. Bake for 25-30 minutes, then cool for 10 minutes.

6. Cut logs into 1/2 inch slices and bake again for 10 minutes on each side until crisp.

Printed in Great Britain
by Amazon

36826940R00040